T0130521

Tips for Managing Your Classroom

Adapted from chapter 4 of
*What to Do with the Kid Who . . . :
Developing Cooperation,
Self-Discipline, and Responsibility
in the Classroom,* 2nd edition.

Kay Burke

CORWIN PRESS
A SAGE Publications Company
Thousand Oaks, California

For information:

Corwin Press
A Sage Publications Company
2455 Teller Road
Thousand Oaks, California 91320
E-mail: order@corwinpress.com

Sage Publications Ltd.
1 Oliver's Yard
55 City Road
London EC1Y 1SP
United Kingdom

Sage Publications India Pvt. Ltd.
B-42, Panchsheel Enclave
Post Box 4109
New Delhi 110 017 India

ISBN 978-1-5751-7441-9

This book is printed on acid-free paper.

09   10   9   8   7   6   5   4

Tips for Managing Your Classroom

Contents

Classroom Climate

Visitors can get a "feel" for a school when they walk down the halls, visit the classrooms, and observe how students and teachers interact. The climate of a school is difficult to define, but educators know it has a tremendous impact on teaching and learning.

In describing the climate of a classroom, educators often begin with a vision of what the classroom ought to be like. The ideal climate promotes deep understanding and excitement about learning. Students take an active role in making some of the decisions about how their classroom will operate. When students are empowered to solve problems, make choices, and provide input into their learning, they assume responsibility for their own classroom community.

Obedience versus Responsibility

The obedience model of classroom management relies on external controlling factors such as authority figures to make students compliant. Kohn (1996) describes how teachers using this model sometimes use a lockstep system of rewards and punishments to ensure students' compliance. This model usually breaks down, however, if the authority figure leaves the room because students do not have any ownership in the system.

Teachers and school programs that practice the responsibility model, however, help students develop their own internal locus of control. Students will exercise self-discipline and behave appropriately because it is the right thing to do—not because they fear getting caught. Figure 1 compares the two models.

Obedience Model vs. Responsibility Model

• Authority figures (external control)	• Self-discipline (internal control)
• Fear of getting caught	• Desire to do the right thing
• Detached	• Involved

Figure 1

Students who feel their opinions are valued become active participants in their own learning process. They care about their fellow students and their classroom community; moreover, they take ownership of their own behavior and learning.

Expectations

Even the most responsible student, however, will not always know what to do in all classroom situations if no one reviews the expectations. If students are not aware of how to move into groups, get the teacher's attention, or obtain supplies, they cannot be expected to perform or behave appropriately. Students need routines or procedures to follow so that the classroom community can operate smoothly and efficiently with a minimum of teacher interventions and time off task.

In the responsibility model, students are involved in establishing the expectations that govern their activities and behaviors. Teachers usually take the lead in determining the key areas that have to be addressed, but they allow students to participate in the process.

It is important to set developmentally appropriate expectations so that students understand how they should behave and are able to comply. One of the major problems involves students who do not receive guidance and modeling of appropriate social behavior from their parents in their early years. If students have not learned to read social cues, form friendships, empathize, and work cooperatively with others from birth, they will have trouble forming relationships when they get to school. The teacher of the twenty-first century cannot assume that every student who walks into his or her classroom has learned how to interact with others. Teaching social skills and helping children develop interpersonal skills are critical tools necessary for success in school and in life. Many state standards address the importance of cooperation, team building, interpersonal relationships, and leadership. These skills need to be taught, re-taught as needed, and practiced since they form the foundation of interactive learning.

Setting Up the Classroom

Scenario

"I feel it is very important that we always walk in the halls and enter the room slowly. Why do you think that procedure is important?" asks Mrs. Saunders.

"I saw a boy get hurt once when another boy was rushing into the room and knocked him into the doorknob real hard," Mary replies.

"I don't like getting shoved by someone who is afraid of being late," adds John.

"So, you think we should all be courteous and enter the room walking rather than running or shoving?" Mrs. Saunders asks.

"Yes," says the class.

"All right, let's practice how we should all enter the room. Everyone file out quietly and stand by the drinking fountain down the hall. When I give the signal, you will all walk towards our classroom and enter the room the way we discussed."

Students rehearse entering the classroom and taking their seat.

"I really liked the way you took turns entering the room and going to your desks. Now, what do you think would be a consequence if someone forgot our procedure and ran into someone while running into the room?"

"I think that person should have to go back and practice walking into the room again just like we practiced today," says Juan.

"He should also have to apologize to who-ever he ran into 'cause no one likes to be pushed," Jack adds.

"Okay," says Mrs. Saunders, "I think we all agree on the importance of this procedure. We'll add this to our list of classroom procedures and consequences we have posted in our room."

Classroom Structure

Few students function well in a chaotic environment. Even though students may think they like having the freedom to do whatever they want, whenever they want, most of them prefer structures, routines, or limits to give them guidance. Structure can be implemented through the arrangement of the classroom, as well as through establishing classroom procedures, rules, and consequences.

Room Arrangement

The proactive teacher anticipates things that can go wrong and attempts to arrange her room, plan her lessons, and practice routines to minimize the amount of downtime that often leads to disruptions. Before students walk into class on the first day of school, teachers can arrange the desks, tables, and chairs to permit orderly movement and to make efficient use of available space.

Evertson, Emmer, Clements, and Worsham (1997) suggest teachers consider the following guidelines when arranging their classrooms:

1. Keep high-traffic areas free of congestion.
2. Be sure students can be seen easily by the teacher.
3. Keep frequently used teaching materials and student supplies readily accessible.

4. Be certain students can easily see whole-class presentations and displays. (pp. 3–4)

Figure 2 shows a room configuration where students face each other for group work. Each student also has a clear view of the teacher, blackboard, and screen. Students who have their backs to the focus activity or the teacher tend to drift off task.

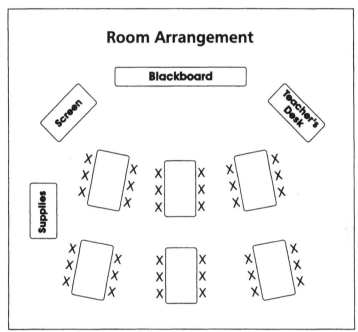

Figure 2

If a room has individual desks rather than tables, teachers have several options. They can separate the desks into rows if the students are listening to a lecture, viewing a video, watching a demonstration, doing quiet seat work, or taking a test. If the lesson involves pairs, triads, or larger groups of four or five, students need to practice moving their desks quickly and quietly into cooperative groups. The movement of desks and the organization of small groups necessitates a procedure that must be taught, practiced, and re-taught until students feel comfortable with the routine. The transition period between activities is often loud and chaotic and allows for "downtime" that could lead to behavior disruptions. When students rehearse how to move themselves and their desks into small- and large-group configurations, however, they establish a routine. They know what they are expected to do, and they do it with little or no prompting and without the teacher having to yell directions over the noise.

Classroom Procedures

In addition to arranging the room and practicing moving into groups, students can be involved in discussing the rationale for establishing other procedures to govern their classroom community. Procedures are routines that need to be taught so that students know what is expected of them. Steps for teaching procedures include the following:

1. Review the procedures with the students.
2. Practice the procedures with the class.
3. Post procedures on the bulletin board.
4. Reteach and rehearse procedures as needed.

Some procedures may be negotiable and others may be nonnegotiable. For example, students cannot decide that coming to class late is an option. They may, however, help determine what the consequences would be if students are repeatedly tardy.

The key to effective procedures is consistency. If a procedure is not working or is developmentally inappropriate, it should be discussed and changed. If the procedure is necessary, however, it should be enforced. A breakdown in classroom management does not usually begin with a bang—it begins with a whimper!

Teachers can review the following list (Figure 3) as a starting point for thinking about which procedures are important to implement in their classrooms.

Classroom Procedures
Do Students Know What Is Expected
of Them for Routine Operations?

Directions: Review the following procedures and check the ones your students will need.

A. Beginning the Class
- ❏ How should students enter the room?
- ❏ What constitutes being late (in the room, in the seat)?
- ❏ How and when will absentee slips be handled?
- ❏ What type of seating arrangements will be used (assigned seats, open seating, cooperative group seating)?
- ❏ How will the teacher get students' attention to start class (the tardy bell, a signal such as a raised hand or lights turned off and on)?
- ❏ How will students behave during Public Address (PA) announcements?

B. Classroom Management
- ❏ How and when will students leave their seats?
- ❏ What do students need in order to leave the room (individual passes, room pass, teacher's permission)?

(continued on the next page)

Figure 3

❏ How will students get help from the teacher (raise hands, put name on board, ask other group members first)?

❏ What are acceptable noise levels for discussion, group work, seat work (six-inch voices)?

❏ How should students work with other students or move into cooperative groups (moving desks, changing seats, noise level, handling materials)?

❏ How will students get recognized to talk (raised hand, teacher calls on student, talk out)?

❏ How do students behave during presentations by other students?

❏ How do students get supplies they are missing?

❏ How and when do students sharpen pencils?

❏ How will students get materials or use special equipment?

C. Paper Work

❏ How will students turn in work (put in specific tray or box, pass to the front, one student collects)?

❏ How will students turn in makeup work if they were absent (special tray, give to teacher, put in folder, give to teacher's aide)?

❏ How will students distribute handouts (first person in row, a group member gets a copy for all group members, students pick up as they enter room)?

❏ How will late work be graded (no penalty, minus points, zero, "F", use lunch or recess to finish, turn in by end of day, drop a certain number of homework grades)?

❏ How and when will students make up quizzes and tests missed (same day they return to school, within twenty-four hours, within the week, before school, during lunch or recess, after school)?

(continued on the next page)

❑ How will late projects such as research papers, portfolios, and artwork be graded (no penalty, minus points, lowered letter grade, no late work accepted)?

D. Dismissal from Class or School

❑ How are students dismissed for lunch?

❑ When do students leave class for the day (when the bell rings, when teacher gives the signal)?

❑ Can students stay after class to finish assignments, projects, tests?

❑ Can the teacher keep one student or the whole class after class or school?

❑ What do students do during fire and disaster drills?

E. Course Outline

❑ How are students made aware of course objectives?

❑ How are students made aware of course requirements?

❑ Are students given due dates for major assignments several weeks in advance?

❑ Are students told how they will be evaluated and given the grading scale?

F. Other Procedures

You may need to introduce procedures related to recess, assemblies, guest speakers, substitute teachers, field trips, teacher leaving the room, etc. List other procedures that could be needed.

_____

_____

_____

_____

The teacher usually knows the types of procedures that will be needed to help the class flow smoothly. It is important, however, to include the students in the discussion and final acceptance of the procedures. Students need to know the rationale for establishing procedures. Once they feel they know the way the class will operate, they feel empowered and are more likely to follow the procedures because they understand the importance of organization in their classroom community.

The students' understanding and acceptance of classroom procedures is just the first step in developing a classroom management plan. Procedures deal with the nuts and bolts, whereas the rules deal with important interpersonal skills that govern how students respect their teachers, interact with their peers, and value themselves and others. Without the organizational framework provided by teaching procedures established at the beginning of the year, teachers will end up sacrificing teaching time to deal with management problems.

Classroom Management

Scenario

"Okay class," begins Mrs. Baker. "I see that one of the rules on our web is 'Listen to others when they are speaking.' Let's talk about that rule before we vote on it."

"I don't like that rule," Mary offers. *"When I get an idea, I have to blurt it out quickly or I'll lose it."*

"Yeah," Sam agrees, "sometimes I'll lose my idea if I wait for someone to stop talking."

"All right, Mary and Sam have some legitimate concerns about the rule. Let's role-play a situation and see if we can get a handle on this problem. I'll start talking about the Middle Ages, and we'll allow students to interrupt when they have an idea.

"One of the major problems confronting the people in the Middle Ages was the Bubonic Plague. Researchers estimate that as many as one-third the population of Europe died because of the plague. One interesting thing about . . ."

"Is that like AIDS today?" Jimmy interrupts.

"Didn't rats spread the plague?" wonders Susan.

"Oh yuck, I hate rats!" shouts Juanita.

"Ooh, I saw a movie about these rats that took over a whole city. It was gross!" Sam adds.

"Well, my sister has a pet rat and he's not gross," Susan retorts.

"Are you kidding? My next-door neighbor has a pet snake. I bet it eats rats!" yells Jimmy.

Finally, Mrs. Baker says, "Umm, let's see. Yes, Jimmy, we are going to talk later about how the plague compares to AIDS, and yes, Susan, the plague was spread by fleas on rats. We'll be talking about that more tomorrow. Let's see, what else?"

"Stop!" yells Mary. "I think I understand why it's bad to interrupt. When people blurt things out, we get off track. Also, it's rude to interrupt our teacher in the middle of her sentence."

"I'm glad you can see how easy it is to get off track when somebody talks in the middle of my idea," says Mrs. Baker.

"I agree," Sam says. "I don't like people interrupting me. I can see how you need to finish your idea and then call on someone. I'll vote for it!"

"Let's take a vote. All those in favor of passing the rule to listen to others without interrupting them, please raise your hand!" says Mrs. Baker.

"Great, 32 in favor; 3 opposed. By virtue of this class meeting, we hereby pass Rule #1. Elsa, please write it on our list on the wall."

Classroom Rules

The classroom procedures provide the framework for organizing a classroom whereas the classroom rules provide the social structure for dealing with people. Classroom rules help govern the social interactions that create a positive learning climate.

Terminology

Jones and Jones (1998) have some concerns about using the term *rules*. They believe the term suggests compliance to classroom management. Therefore, they suggest instead using terms such as *behavioral standards, norms, expectations,* or *principles* to "describe the agreements teachers and students make regarding the types of behaviors that help a classroom be a safe community of support" (p. 241).

Guidelines

Regardless of the terminology used, students need to be involved in the process. Discipline based on discussion and consensus is more effective than the totalitarian approach captured by this cartoon where the teacher makes all the rules.

"I only have one class rule . . . 'What I say goes'."

First published in *Phi Delta Kappan,* December 1997.

Curwin and Mendler (1988) believe there is a "delicate balance between meeting the needs of the group by maintaining social order and meeting the unique needs of each student" (p. 20). Rules can help maintain social order. They are usually more effective if they:

1. provide guidelines,
2. are stated clearly,
3. are stated positively,
4. adhere to school rules, and
5. are limited to five.

Rules that describe behavior norms enable students to understand what is expected of them. If rules are too specific, however, too many rules are needed. For example:

Too specific: "Students should not borrow, steal, deface, damage, or lose the property of others."
Better rule: "Students should respect the property of others."

Other rules or principles that set expectations for student behavior include the following:

1. Respect the dignity of all adults and students.
2. Respect the opinions of others.
2. Respect the property of others.
3. Be polite, courteous, and caring.
5. Participate in your own learning.

A set of five rules are sufficient to cover most classroom behaviors, but teachers sometimes need to add a new rule to cover a problem behavior when it occurs.

Teaching the Rules

It is imperative that students get an opportunity to discuss the proposed classroom rules and understand the rationale behind them. A class meeting is the perfect opportunity to have a frank discussion of the rules, role-play situations, and come to a class consensus about the rules the students and teacher will adopt to ensure a positive classroom environment.

It is important to note that some rules just like some procedures are nonnegotiable. Students must understand that the school district or the school sets rules that are not subject to a vote. Rules related to fighting, damage to property, injury to self or others, and weapons set parameters to ensure the health and safety of all students. It is important that teachers review school rules and the discipline policies with students during the first few days of class to make sure they understand them. Many times students are required to sign a statement acknowledging their understanding of the rules and the consequences they will face if they violate them.

Consequences

After class members and the teacher agree on their classroom rules, they also need to discuss and agree on the logical consequences students will face if they violate them. The obedience model paradigm of teachers dictating all the rules and determining the punishments is no longer effective. Reliance on threat and intimidation and the "fear factor" erodes a positive classroom climate. Student involvement in the organization of the classroom models the democratic process.

Some discipline programs use consequences as punitive revenge on students. Kohn (1996) says that an intervention could qualify as a punishment if it is deliberately chosen to be be unpleasant. "A punishment makes somebody suffer in order to teach a lesson" (p. 24). For example, if a student bites another student, he has to wear a sign saying "I bite people." If a student writes notes, she has to read them in front of the class. Curwin and Mendler (1988) warn that "a consequence can become a punishment if it is delivered aggressively" (p. 65). Consequences are most effective if they are clear, consistent, logical, and easy to enforce.

If a student violates the rule about not completing homework, the consequence would not logically be to send that student to the principal. The consequence would more logically involve having the student turn in the homework before the end of the day, stay in from recess or lunch to finish it, or lose points on his grade. Consequences should relate directly to the rule violation. Consequences such as "sit in the corner," "go to the office," or write "I will not talk" 500 times do not fit the crime.

In addition, punishments or consequences administered as punishments often diminish the dignity of the student as well as breed resentment and resistance. Punishment teaches a student what he is *not* supposed to do, instead of teaching him what he *is* supposed to do. Glasser (1992) warns that students will not be coerced into doing anything. Students must see the rationale behind the rules and they must be a part of the process. They should also be allowed to make a few mistakes. Students forget and they get confused, especially if they have to follow different rules in each class.

Some global consequences include those outlined in Figure 4. Other consequences could be more specifically related to the rule (see Figure 5).

Offense and Consequence

First offense	Gentle reminder (Many student simply forget to follow the rule.)
Second offense	Second reminder (The rule has not yet become a routine.)
Third offense	Conference with student to discuss the problem
Fourth offense	Social contract with student to solve the problem
Fifth offense	Conference with parent, counselor, or administrator to address solutions to the problem

---

Figure 4

Examples

Rule	Consequences
Students will respect the opinions of others.	1. Reminder 2. Second reminder 3. Student must meet with student he or she insulted. 4. Social contract 5. Conference with parent 6. Conference with counselor
Rule	**Consequences**
Students must participate in their own learning.	1. Reminder 2. Conference with student 3. Student must stay in from recess or after school to complete work. 4. Points subtracted from grade 5. Conference with parent 6. Conference with counselor or administrator

Figure 5

If students have some input in the establishment of the consequences, they are more likely to accept them. Furthermore, teachers need to administer the consequences calmly and fairly. They should remind students privately that they still like and respect the student as a person—it is his or her actions that are unacceptable. Students who realize they have not fulfilled their responsibility or obligation are likely to accept their consequences as long as they are treated with respect. Students also prefer to talk privately with the teacher rather than have peers or the entire class witness the verbal exchange.

Behavior Checklists

Hopefully, students will accept the "rule and consequence" paradigm, take responsibility for their actions, and model exemplary behavior. (We can always hope!) The need still exists, however, for teachers to chronicle the behavior of those who choose not to cooperate in order to document the students' lack of progress.

Teachers use grade books, checklists, or anecdotal records to record disruptive behavior. Writing the names of misbehaving students on the blackboard and adding checks after their names for repeat offenses, however, is not conducive to establishing classroom trust, nor does it build the self-esteem of students. It is important to avoid public confrontations and power struggles with students, especially when the whole class is watching.

Teachers do not want to take time away from academics to keep track of discipline violations, but there are ways teachers can monitor student behavior efficiently. The checklist (see Figure 6) helps teachers keep track of violations without publicly embarrassing students or losing instructional time. It is suggested that teachers record specific dates under each rule violation to determine which consequence applies and to document reoccurring discipline problems.

Accurate record keeping is important because many students are totally unaware that they are violating the rules. Moreover, they often have no idea they are repeatedly violating the rule. Sometimes the documentation of the dates helps make them aware of their chronic misbehavior. Accurate records are also necessary for referrals, conferences with parents and administrators, and more serious interventions such as detentions, in-house suspensions, or formal hearings.

Behavior Checklist

Teacher: _Burke_   Class: _American Lit_   Date: _10/5_

Rules: Consequences:
Rule #1 _Respect the property of others_   1. _Reminder_
Rule #2 _Respect other's opinions_   2. _Warning_
Rule #3 _Honor assignment deadlines_   3. _Teacher-Student Conference_
Rule #4 _Participate in your learning_   4. _Social Contract_
Rule #5 _Cooperate with peers_   5. _Conference with parent_

Write the dates of all violations in boxes under rule numbers.

Class Roll	Rule					Comments
3rd Period	1	2	3	4	5	
1. Carol					9/9	changed her group
2. Pat			9/15			
3. Lois						
4. Mike						
5. Terry	9/13	9/14	9/15	9/22	9/29	conference with parent
6. Michael						
7. Havali						
8. Kevin			9/15			gave him calendar
9. Kathy						
10. Sharon						
11. Rich						
12. Tommy						
13. Jose						
14. Sean						
15. Mary Lou						
16. Colleen						
17. Kayla						
18. Pauline						
19. Merrill						
20. Jeff	10/3	9/15	9/21			conference with student

Figure 6

28

A checklist is one method to monitor improper student behavior. Other methods include logs, journals, anecdotal records, and social contracts. Regardless of the method used, it is important to keep accurate records in order to document the teacher's attempts to address the problems and to support discussions in student and parent conferences.

♪♪♪ *I'm making a list, checking it twice . . .*
gonna find out who's naughty or nice . . . ♪♪♪

First printed in *Designing Professional Portfolios for Change Training Manual* (Burke 1997).

A Cooperative Classroom

Scenario

"I hate doing these geometry problems," groans Chuck. "Why do we need to know this for life? We spend half the class working on these theorems!"

"What's the problem, Chuck?" asks Mrs. Nordstrom.

"Math is boring," Chuck explodes.

"Now, Chuck," Mrs. Nordstrom replies, "things are not boring—people who don't understand them just think they're boring."

"I understand the problems," shouts Chuck. "I just don't give a damn!"

"If you understand so much," says Mrs. Nordstrom through gritted teeth, her voice rising, "Why did you score a 54 percent on your last test?"

"Because I wanted to flunk—it was my personal best."

"You'll never get into college."

"So what?" yells Chuck. "I hate this class and I hate you!"

"Alright, young man. You can just march yourself down to the principal's office right now," Mrs. Nordstrom screams.

"Great. I'd rather sit in his office all day than listen to you!"

The Value of Respect

Kohl (as cited in Scherer 1998) believes that one of the greatest influences on classroom management is respect. If teachers do not feel that their students have equal value to themselves, then they will not teach them much. Kohl also believes that humiliation is absolutely a sin. He feels that teachers need to deal with students who defy them, but humiliation has to go.

Publicly humiliating or embarrassing students does not help students learn from their mistakes. It could, however, make them try harder not to get caught and cause them to devise clever ways to get revenge on whoever embarrassed them. They may also seek revenge on the whole class or student body who witnessed their public humiliation. Recent incidents of violence in schools attests to the power of revenge.

Dealing with disruptive students in private, in a fair and consistent manner, and in a manner that maintains their dignity and self-esteem helps them develop an internal locus of control and responsibility. Students with an internal locus of control feel guilty when they misbehave, learn from their mistakes, accept the consequences for their actions, and control their actions in the future.

Dealing with disruptive students in front of their peers in an emotional outburst of frustration and anger lowers the students' self-concept. It also decreases their desire to cooperate and succeed and prevents them from developing their own sense of responsibility. Students learn how to become defensive and use their external locus of control to blame others for their problems. Consequently, these students rarely accept responsibility for their own actions. Public reprimands, moreover, eventually destroy the positive climate in any classroom. Students do not feel free to engage in interactive discussion, contribute ideas, or share experiences if they are never sure when their teacher will ridicule or insult them. Teachers who model respect for their students will often receive the students' respect in return.

Coercive Teacher Behaviors

If students perceive that the teacher is treating them unjustly, they may label that teacher "unfair" or "the enemy." The seeds of insurrection may then be planted, causing a small behavior incident to escalate into a major discipline problem that lasts the whole year.

Teachers need to self-regulate their enforcement of classroom rules and consequences. Sometimes the message can be fair, consistent, and positive, but the delivery system can be sarcastic, punitive, and negative.

The "Dirty Dozen" (see Figure 7) describes teacher behaviors that can erode a positive classroom climate and undermine any discipline program—no matter how democratic. Teachers can send signals to individual students and to the whole class in both subtle and blatant ways that jeopardize the caring, cooperative classroom. It is remarkable how many people remember an incident from school in which they were treated unjustly. These incidents often become a defining moment in shaping their own character.

Every teacher has violated or will violate one of the dirty dozen on some occasions. Everyone has bad days—including teachers. The key is to reduce or eliminate the types of teacher behaviors that cause students to shut down, drop out, or resort to fight or flight to save face. Students who have not come from a nurturing home environment where they learned empathy, self-control, and respect need an adult to model those traits.

Burke's "Dirty Dozen"

1.	**Sarcasm**	Students' feelings can be hurt by sarcastic put-downs thinly disguised as humor.
2.	**Negative tone of voice**	Students can read between the lines and sense a sarcastic, negative, or condescending tone of voice.
3.	**Negative body language**	A teacher's clenched fists, set jaw, quizzical look, or threatening stance can speak more loudly than any words.
4.	**Inconsistency**	Nothing escapes the students' attention. They are the first to realize the teacher is not enforcing the rules and consequences consistently.
5.	**Favoritism**	Brownnosing is an art and any student in any class can point out the teacher's pet who gets special treatment.
6.	**Put-downs**	Sometimes teachers are not aware they are embarrassing a student with subtle put-downs or insults.
7.	**Outbursts**	Teachers are sometimes provoked by students and they "lose it." These teacher outbursts set a bad example for the students and could escalate into more serious problems.
8.	**Public reprimands**	No one wants to be corrected, humiliated, or lose face in front of his or her peers.
9.	**Unfairness**	Taking away promised privileges, scheduling a surprise test, nitpicking while grading homework or tests, or assigning punitive homework could be construed as unfair.
10.	**Apathy**	Students do not want to be ignored. Teachers who forget students' names or appear indifferent will lose students' respect.
11.	**Inflexibility**	Teachers who never adjust homework assignments or test dates to meet the needs of their students appear rigid and uncaring.
12.	**Lack of humor**	Teachers who cannot laugh at themselves usually do not encourage students to take risks and make mistakes. Humorless classes lack energy.

Figure 7

34

The teacher is the architect who designs the microworld of the classroom. The values, attitudes, and social skills the teacher models sets the tone for the class.

Proactive Teachers

The effective classroom teacher engages in a professional response to a student's inappropriate action or comment. The teacher models the rule, "Respect the dignity of others." Proactive teachers also prevent discipline problems before they occur rather than always reacting to them after they develop. Teachers can utilize the following strategies to engage in a proactive approach to preventing behavior problems.

1. Anticipate potential behavior problems.
   - Assign potential problem students to different groups.
   - Arrange seating patterns so teacher can see and be close to misbehaving students.
   - Provide both verbal and written directions to eliminate confusion and frustration.
   - Structure assignments that are relevant, motivating, and developmentally appropriate.
   - Allow enough time for students to complete assignments.
   - Scan the class frequently to monitor potential problems.
   - Engage in private conversations to discover students' personal or family problems.
   - Make allowances for students with learning disabilities or physical handicaps so they are not overwhelmed.
   - Encourage peer tutoring so students can help each other.

- Talk with counselors or support personnel to find out about any previous behavior problems students might have experienced and get suggestions about how to best meet the individual needs of students.

2. Diffuse minor problems before they become major disturbances.

Proximity

- Move close to students to monitor their actions.
- Make eye contact with misbehaving student.

Student-Selected Time-Out

- Allow the agitated student go to a desk or chair in the corner of the room to collect his or her thoughts or calm down.

Teacher-Selected Time-Out

- Ask the student to go to the time-out area to complete work when his or her behavior is disrupting the class.

3. Address disruptive behaviors immediately.

- Speak with the student privately in the hall, after class, or after school.
- Ask the student to explain what he or she thinks the problem is.
- Send "I-messages" telling the student how his or her behavior affects you. For example, "I feel upset when I see you arguing with your group members because you won't complete the assignment."
- Identify the real problem. Sometimes the student's reading problem is preventing him or her from doing the work.
- Remind students of the procedures or rules.
- Address the problem quickly, calmly, and confidentially.

- Do not create a bigger class disruption when attempting to solve problems.
- Avoid outbursts.
- Remove the offender from the class so he or she does not have an audience.
- Provide students with choices. For example, "If you choose to work alone rather than with your group, you must complete the entire project by yourself."

Proactive teachers avoid many potential problems. Teachers who can not anticipate problems spend too much time *reacting* to problems. The key to successful classroom management is prevention—and prevention should begin the first minute of the first day of class.

The Last Resort: The Principal

Even if teachers are proactive, there will always be one or more students who choose to disrupt the rest of the class because the class does not satisfy their needs. Their need for attention, power, or recognition supersedes their need to learn or their desire to cooperate.

It is the teacher's responsibility to make sure these disruptive students do not destroy the positive atmosphere of the class. If teachers do their best to anticipate potential behavior problems, diffuse minor problems before they become major disturbances, and address disruptive behaviors immediately, they should be able to manage most problems. Once the teacher has done everything possible to solve the problem, however, he or she must resort to outside help—the administration. Sending the student to the principal is not a cop-out or a sign of teacher inadequacy, unless, of course, it is done at the first sign of a problem or for minor infractions.

Teachers who relinquish the position of authority early on in a problem situation with a student will lose not only the respect of that student but also the respect of the class. Once the teacher turns over the problem to the administrator, he or she is no longer in control. If, however, the teacher has exhausted his or her repertoire of strategies, the student's behavior has not improved, and the negative behavior is disrupting the entire class, the last resort becomes the next step. The student may need to be referred to the school counselor, psychologist, special education coordinator, or social worker. It is important that teachers have accurate documentation of the student's behavior (dates, incidents, actions taken, checklists, referrals) so administrators know the teacher has taken many steps to help the student succeed.

The problem-solving strategies that teachers utilize to address behavior problems don't always work. Effective teachers, however, are always searching for strategies to meet the needs of all their students. Teaching is a learning experience and this week's challenge often becomes next week's triumph.

References

Burke, K. 2000. *What to do with the kid who . . .: Developing cooperation, self-discipline, and responsibility in the classroom,* 2nd ed. Arlington Heights, IL: SkyLight Training and Publishing.

Burke, K. 1997. *Designing professional portfolios for change training manual.* Arlington Heights, IL: SkyLight Training and Publishing.

Curwin, R. L, and A. N. Mendler. 1988. *Discipline with dignity.* Alexandria, VA: Association for Supervision and Curriculum Development.

Evertson, C. M., E. T. Emmer., B. S. Clements, and M. E. Worsham. 1997. *Classroom management for elementary teachers,* 4th ed. Boston: Allyn & Bacon.

Glasser, W. 1992. *The quality school: Managing students without coercion.* 2nd ed., expanded. New York: Harper Perennial.

Jones, V. F., and L. S. Jones. 1998. *Comprehensive classroom management: Creating communities of support and solving problems,* 5th ed. Boston: Allyn & Bacon.

Kohn, A. 1996. *Beyond discipline: From compliance to community.* Alexandria, VA: Association for Supervision and Curriculum Development.

Scherer, M. 1998. The discipline of hope: A conversation with Herb Kohl. *Educational Leadership* 56(1): 8–13.

**CORWIN
PRESS**

The Corwin Press logo—a raven striding across an open book—
represents the union of courage and learning. Corwin Press is committed
to improving education for all learners by publishing books and other
professional development resources for those serving the field of PreK–12
education. By providing practical, hands-on materials, Corwin Press
continues to carry out the promise of its motto: **"Helping Educators Do
Their Work Better."**

Printed in the United States
By Bookmasters